TELL ME ABOUT
YOURSELF

Keys for Adulting Beginners

Seeking to CrossOver

SIMA BALLINGER

Tell Me About Yourself

Keys for Adulting Beginners Seeking to CrossOver

This is a work of non-fiction.

Printed in the United States of America

First paperback edition August 2020

ISBN: 978-1-7355038-0-6

Publisher: Sima Ballinger

248.205.9423

Southfield, Michigan

Dedication

This book is dedicated to my husband, Marvin Ballinger, who has been my rock, strength and support. My beautiful adult children, Virginia [Married to Marjace], Benjamin and Jasper, who are the loves of my life. I also dedicate this book in memory of my mother, the late Vera Beard, and father, the late Rev. Dr. Lessley Beard—their teachings remain in me. My dear sister, Andrea Lynn Dudley [Michael her husband], for her love and motivation. My late brothers, Lessley Beard and Ronald Beard, Rest In Peace. And my church family, Family Victory Fellowship, for their encouragement. Above all, I thank God for being my source of power and guiding my footsteps. He is my all and all.

Contents

INTRODUCTION

Before I completed this manuscript, I always wanted to write a book, and it was suggested to me several years ago to share my wisdom. I have been writing as a freelancer for many years and have written well over 700 articles online. So, when COVID-19 pandemic struck, I found myself in a bedroom that I had converted into an office on the second floor of my home to write what was on my heart. Almost everywhere I looked there was a sign to write a book. So, I decided to get my thoughts out of my head and put them on paper.

I had a wonderful childhood, but there was one key ingredient missing. Most of the time, I was told what to do. I was not asked what I wanted or my opinion, and maybe the same for you as well. So, I came up with the title, Tell Me About Yourself, Keys for Adulting Beginners Seeking to CrossOver. This book is intended to help young people become adults and learn sooner than later about themselves and their capabilities.

My husband and I have raised three fine adult children of whom we are very proud: a daughter and two sons. Two are college graduates, one of whom is working on a second degree. The other son is a Sergeant in the United States Army and has served five years as a service member. We have given our children a respectable life. And we are small business owners in our community and serve the community at large.

The main thing I want this book to do is to motivate you to bring whatever gift or talent you have to the table and develop it into something great. No gift is too small when it is given with love and the right motivation. As a young girl, I recall winning 1st place in a Spelling Bee Contest, and that was my cue that there was something inside of me to do something great. The girl that I was in competition with, in the final round, is an executive and attorney today.

You Have a Seat at the Table

Young people all over the land and country, I hear you loud and clear, so take your seat at the table. I am listening to your cry, and you send a resounding message of hope and change. Older people, elders, preachers, teachers and especially parents, guide and hold the hand of the young people in your life. Young people born between 1981 – 1996 are the millennials that will carry this nation and move our country forward. As protesters and drumbeats for justice and equality, they will make change come and make our world a better place to live in for *all* people. While America is in the throes of a pandemic and suffering racial injustice at the death of George Floyd, many opportunities will manifest in the land.

I am writing to the young man who lost a parent and has financial challenges. I am writing to the young girl who has made some bad choices but wants to make real change in her life. I am writing to young people who have skills that are not being utilized in the right industry. I am writing to young people who have lost hope and do not know which way to turn. And lastly, I am writing to young people who are on a good trajectory for success.

Pull Up a Chair

The chair is three-fold and is symbolic of learning, leading and lending. When you are seated in a chair in the classroom, you are there to learn. When you are at a meeting, sitting at the head of the table, you are there to lead. And when you are seated elsewhere in the room, you are there to lend... your thoughts, a helping hand, or some type of assistance. The roles should always be in motion in your life. Sometimes, you are learning, sometimes, you are leading, and sometimes, you are lending.

Learning

Do you need more training, college or to attend a trade school to improve your abilities? Learning is the foundation for growth. You must be humble to learn. You must submit yourself to someone who has the capability to teach you what you do not know. Often, the person who can help you grow the most is your parent. The first step in growing is submitting and honoring your parent. If you have trouble submitting to your parent, you will have a problem learning. You will not be able to get around learning to get where you want to go. The greatest leaders of our time were taught by someone.

Tiger Woods, a world-famous golfer, was trained by his father. Mark Zuckerberg, Facebook CEO, as a youngster, had a private tutor, David Newman, to teach him the computer. Venus and Serena Williams, world-famous tennis players, were initially trained by their parents. After high school, Barack Obama, first Black President and 44th president of the United States, received his education at Occidental College, Columbia University and Harvard Law School.

Leading

When you are sitting at the head of the table in the lead role, calling the shots, you better have your head on straight. You have people depending on you and your ability to make good decisions. To be a leader, you must hold yourself to a higher standard than your peers and cohorts. If the store opens at 10:00 am, you need to be there before 10:00am. You need to arrive in enough time to greet your staff and those who are depending on you. That is right, when you are a leader, you are a humble servant. And you *need* the followers to accomplish your mission.

Lending

It is important to lend yourself to someone, in other words, volunteer. When a protest is going on, most of the people in the group are lenders. Lenders participate, they follow instructions and band together to create a cohesive front. There is a plethora of things that you can lend: your time, your ear, your thoughts, and your financial support. Proverbs 19:17 (AMP), He who is gracious *and* lends a hand to the poor lends to the Lord, And the Lord will repay him for his good deed.

So, here is our chance to show each other that we can change the world with this one book. As you think about yourself or your children through the enclosed topics, my hope is that you will discover a part of you that you never knew before. In every chapter, there are several keys to unlock your potential, and as you read, you will discover them. Enjoy the facts, the stories, and the few exercises, and take a journey to CrossOver.

Where there is no revelation, people cast off restraint; but blessed is the one who heeds wisdom's instruction. – Proverbs 29:18

CHAPTER ONE

Tell Me About Your Big Impossible
Dream (Vision)

Just because a man lacks the use of his eyes doesn't

mean he lacks vision – Stevie Wonder

S tevie Wonder, Multi-Grammy winner, Pop and R&B singer, songwriter and musician lacks sight, but not vision. Although Stevie Wonder is blind, he does not lack the ability to dream big. He will go down in history as one of the greatest singers of our time. Wonder's songs have reached millions. You have probably heard some of his songs, "Isn't She Lovely," "You Are the Sunshine of My Life," "My Eyes Don't Cry No More." I believe that his ability to imagine is enhanced because of his lack of sight. Have you ever wondered why dreaming is associated with having your eyes closed? It is said that when you have no sight, your other senses are heightened. You are keener on moving distractions out of your way. And it is my recommendation that, as you read the content in this book, you block out any distractions. The content herein has the power to change your life. You must believe this to get the most out of it. Once you have internalized your vision, you must write it down.

In the Bible, it says to write the vision and make it plain so that they who read it will run with it – Habakkuk 2:2. A vision is something like having a dream. It is your thoughts and ideas on how you can change the world. A vision is something that you are passionate about. Basically, it is something bigger than your ability. I love to talk about Helen Keller, another blind inspiration, the lady who was deaf and blind; she had no sight, but she had *vision*. The saying goes, it is better to have vision with no sight; than to have sight but no vision. Helen Keller wanted to do something that was, what seemed impossible, to speak. What is the thing in your life that you want to do that seems impossible? The Bible says that with God, all things are possible. Do you have faith to do the impossible?

Even a child can have a vision. A two-year-old sets out to ride a two-wheel bicycle but does not have the ability yet. One way to make the impossible happen is to start with baby steps. In this scenario, the toddler would start out by riding with training wheels. Do you know what training wheels are? They are additional wheels that you put on the outside of the back wheel to support the bicycle. See how easy that was, it is not difficult to accomplish great things in life, it is how you go about doing it. But you must step out and look for ways to cause your breakthrough to come to pass.

Your vision could be something that other people do, and you desire to do as well, such as getting a college degree. Some college students start out at a two-year college before they attend a university. Many people start out in college and do not complete getting their degree because they took on too much. Some people are even given full-ride scholarships because they show great aptitude to succeed. The point is, you can accomplish great things if you start with baby steps and stick with it.

Michelle Obama Admired

I can think of many people in the world who have made a global impact and have done some tremendous things. Michelle Obama is one of those individuals. In a worldwide survey polled by YouGov in 2019, Michelle Obama was found to be the *most admired* woman in the world! Michelle Obama was the first lady of the United States when her husband, Barack Obama, the first black president ever, was in office. It is so easy to talk about Michelle. She conducted herself in a most remarkable way. Her mannerisms, her smile, her dress, her love for her family and her husband was stellar. She is an educated woman as well, with a law degree. And she inspired the world through her initiative to make us all more health conscious. Before Michelle Obama became the first lady of the United States, she may not have had a vision for the White House per se, but she did have a yearning to help people improve their lives. It *is* possible to have a vision without knowing exactly how you will carry it out. I believe one of the main aspects to accomplish a vision is to have your heart right. The Bible says to create in me a clean heart oh God and renew the right spirit within. Psalm 51:10. And once you have this clean heart, you begin to be open to great possibilities. Following the closing of Barack Obama's second term in office as President of the United States, Michelle's book, "Becoming," took off like wildfire and sold more than 10 million units within the first five months on the market, according to the Washington Post.

Do not think that you must be super talented to have a vision. All you need is a thought or an idea

to want to make a difference in your immediate surroundings. Before my husband opened the only
black-owned hobby store in our city, he had a dream
of helping men do something constructive. Growing
up in a two-family flat in an urban area with seven
brothers, he fully understood the need to keep boys
entertained. He tells stories of how he and his brothers used to make a big mess in the house when his
parents were away. At times, they were very de-
structive. But the best times were when they were
rewarded with balsa wood airplanes. He used to
look forward to getting those planes as simple as
they were. That little plane gave him hope and inspiration enough to have his own hobby store.

All you need is a little spark to get the fire going.
One day, my mother put a paddle ball in my hand
that she had purchased at the five and dime store.
And from that one small seed, it gave me hope,

much like my husband. At our hobby store, we do not only sell products, but we also give hope. We plant seeds in our patron's lives for a better tomorrow. It amazes me how God put us together for a great cause. It is a dream come true! So, do not take anything lightly that has happened in your life because one day, it has the potential to change lives, give inspiration and help you CrossOver.

Write Your Vision – The Impossible Dream

_____

_____

_____

It always seems impossible until it gets done! - Nelson Mandela

A good name is more desirable than great riches; to be esteemed is better than silver or gold. – Proverbs 22:1

CHAPTER TWO

Tell Me the Meaning of Your
Name – Who Are You

———————◇———————

T ime to get reacquainted with yourself. From the very day you were born until right now, this very moment, defines you. Start with your name. What is your full name, and what does it mean? I have a rare and unusual name. My father named me Sima, which means treasure. But it was not until I was about 43 years old that I learned what it means. Many years were lost without my knowledge of this powerful meaning of my name.

My world changed when I discovered its meaning. I started sharing my newfound knowledge with everyone. In fact, my value increased immediately. Once you discover the meaning of your name, you will get an immediate ego boost. You will be just like NIKE, ready to "Just Do It."

Another important factor about your birth is to know your biological parents. Having the knowledge of your birth mother and birth father will give you peace and a sense of pride. If you were adopted, your adoptive parents love you and care for you, so tread lightly on this sensitive topic. Talk openly and honestly with your parent about your birth to get an understanding and clarity about your biological parents. Discussing your origin is healthy and will help you CrossOver in a huge way.

Place of Birth

Were you born in a large city, small town, country or rural area? And what is the name of the hospital where you were born? Or perhaps you had a midwife and was born at home. If you do not know the name of your birth hospital, please ask someone. Everything about your birth location adds meaning to your very existence. Knowledge is power. The environment and surroundings in which you were born will follow you for the rest of your days. When you are out of town, people ask you where you are from for a reason. They will ask, "Where are you from?" It is your time to shine when you answer this question. And you will answer cheerfully, "I'm from the rural town of ------- where they make the best cherry pie in the whole world." Well, I made that up, but you understand the significance. The better you can tell your story, the better your chance of getting the right fit opportunities.

Date of Birth

The time of year your mother gave birth to you is also important. In America, we celebrate the four seasons categorized as Winter, Spring, Summer and Fall (Autumn). Therefore, if you were born during June, July and August, you're considered a Summer Baby. Born September, October and November equal a Fall Baby. And for birth in December, January and February, you got it, you're a Winter Baby. Finally, if you are born in the month of March, April and May, you are a Spring Baby. People born in the Spring bring in the warm season, and that is why we are loved so much. So, when were you born, and what is unique about the month you were born?

Parents and Siblings

The size of your family impacts your very existence. Take the McGhee family for example. When they were born, they posted a cute photo of the babies that went viral. The McGhees consists of four boys and two girls. The whole dynamics of six children born the same day seems unreal. The family must go to great lengths to ensure that everyone's needs get met. If you were a guest in their home, you might see things labeled with the names of each child on them so that there will not be any confusion. And the family must be efficient to keep their living expenses affordable. Children born under these circumstances are probably very organized team players.

If you are an only child, your lifestyle probably looks a little different from a full house of children.

Your house may be quieter and less cluttered. You may have even felt lonely more often. On the up-side, you might be spoiled and can get what you want most of the time.

So, where do you fit in your family's birth order? I am the second and being second has certain stig-mas associated with it. When you are not the first, you do not get as much attention as the firstborn in-itially. You may get overlooked often, called "shy," or suffer from low self-esteem. When the firstborn is an extrovert and very outgoing, you must contend with that. The positive side of being second-born is that you get the opportunity to learn from your older sibling's mistakes. You are a good observation learner; you realize that you do not have to experi-ence things to learn a lesson. And if your older sib-ling is like my sister, you are protected and cared for.

Now, if you are in a family of four, the second and third are considered the middle children. And the last child is the youngest, or we also refer to this child as the baby of the family. All the youngest or baby children of the family that I know are amazing. I come from a family of four siblings, but the family size has decreased since I was born. The average number of people per family in the United States in 1960 was 3.7 and in 2019 it consists of 3.14 persons, according to Statista.com.

The Bible says in Psalm 127:5 (NKJV), "Behold, children are a heritage from the Lord, the fruit of the womb a reward. Like arrows in the hand of a warrior are the children of one's youth. Blessed is the man who fills his quiver with them!"

Childhood Lessons Stick with
You throughout Life

When you think about your mother's character traits, what are the skills that draw people to her? What are the skills that she used to persuade you to get something done? The reason I brought your mother into the conversation is that your character is a lot like hers. People say it all the time, "You sound just like your mother." These same character-istics can be thought about for fathers as well.

As I think of my childhood observing my amaz-ing mother in action, I can identify 10 traits that she possessed, which contributed to my success. Note: If you were adopted, in the Adoption Study on Per-sonality, the conclusion of nature vs. nurture, nature wins, biological traits are more prevalent. However, parenting does factor into raising children. Here is the list, see if any of the traits resonate with you.

1. Kind. The entire universe loved my mother. She was very approachable with her gentle ways. She was a giving person, and people loved to be in her midst. The words that came out of her mouth were always words of encouragement, comfort and love. Even though she was kind, she also displayed tough love when needed.

2. Humorous. Laughter was my mother's ace card. Amid drama, sadness or upheaval, she had a way of centering family and friends, thereby creating a sense of security. And this ability to create fun and energy came naturally to her. When she spoke at church and women's events, she shared stories that were

heartfelt and downright funny. At the beginning of her speeches, she always stated that she was not going to be long.

3. Researcher. I enjoy telling stories about observing my mother. I used to watch her study early in the morning when I would be headed out for school after she had prepared breakfast for my father. She would have her books spread out across the kitchen table with her eyeglasses available to grab when needed. She was always gathering information to use in speeches and to share with those in need of counsel.

4. Speaker. My mother was the First Lady of the church that my father pastored and was often requested to speak at events. She was a leader in the community, and other women looked

up to her. It was fascinating to watch her present a speech. Her 10 minute speeches would always be power-packed. She would make you laugh, cry and think, all at the same time. I always gave her a standing ovation every time she spoke. She appeared to be shy, but that was her humility. My sister became a great speaker, as well.

5. Concise. My mother was efficient, not wasteful. She wrote her speeches in cursive on lined 5" x 7" white paper. She lived her life with purpose, and she always had structure built into her day. Her talks were very clear and understandable. She was easy to follow.

6. Smile. My mother was a smiler if there is such a word. She never wore a frown. A smile does not cost you anything but can bring you great benefits. When you take a photograph,

the photographer always says, "Smile." A smile is uplifting, and it shows your inner beauty. A smile is the outward expression of your inner beauty. It is the universal language of peace, joy and love. Funny thing is, she did not like to be photographed. I think it was because she was a full-figured woman. My mother was a plus-sized woman who looked good in her attire from head to toe. She was 5' 2". She would always say that she was "pleasingly plump."

7. Attire. Whenever my mom went to an outing or event, she dressed up with style. She cleaned up real nice. Since she had many engagements, she always had to refresh her wardrobe. My dad made sure that she wore quality clothing, hats, and carried nice handbags. People take notice when your threads

are of good quality; they will take notice, as well, when they are not.

8. Writer. My mother's smooth writing ability preceded her speaking ability. Taking pen to paper was easy for my mother. Well, I never asked her if writing was easy for her; I just know the finished product came out like a best-selling author. I wonder why she never wrote a book. She certainly had the ability and the content.

9. Counselor. Being a counselor is one of the most intriguing skills that my mom possessed. She was a great listener, and when you listen well, people talk. When you are trying to help someone, that person needs you to pay attention. Being on the listening end,

you can provide help and support to the person in need. People were always around her, asking for advice of some kind or another.

10. Wisdom. Finally, is wisdom. My mother was an advocate for reading and studying the Bible. Yes, that is the book for me. You cannot get wisdom from training or sitting in a class, it is given from God, the creator. As you can see, every one of them has the power to add to your bottom line. So, go for it, and select one or two and let them help you CrossOver.

Note: The meaning of baby names is the single most important influence on the development of your baby's personality.

– SelfGrowth.com

What Does Your Name Mean – Etymology of Your Name

_____

_____

_____

_____

_____

_____

Dishonest money dwindles away, but whoever gathers money little by little makes it grow. – Proverbs 13:11

CHAPTER THREE

Tell Me About Your Money Habits

———————○———————

I t may seem obvious, but one of the first rules of money is, do not spend more than you make. Using credit cards can exacerbate your situation. Some employers do a credit check before hiring you, and if it is in bad shape, then you may lose the opportunity. Know your rights about credit checks. Credit scores range from 300 – 850, with 700 being good. To live a comfortable life, you need to know how much money you need to earn a living. Many people cannot honestly say how much they need because they do not have a budget. Images of people and celebrities that you see on television are often hype and do not necessarily represent the individual's true status. Take the celebrity in the lavish home, with a fleet of cars and wardrobe taking up a full room, it looks amazing, but do not be deceived because they could be on the verge of bankruptcy. According to Businessinsider.com, rapper, actor and businessman, "50 Cent" Curtis Jackson, reportedly was in debt of $32.5 million in 2015, and declared bankruptcy in 2016. Good thing he is very talented and can recover to a full state of financial prosperity.

You Can Decide the Income You Want

Your value is not determined or based on how much you make, but it is based on what you *do* with what you make. People do all kinds of crazy things with money. They throw it away by gambling, buy luxury items they do not need, and pay high-interest credit card rates. Financial Guru, Dr. Lynn Richardson recommends you follow the 10/10/30/50 rule, "10% tithe, 10% save, 30% cash in your pocket and 50% stays in your account for bills," Blackenterprise.com. As you can see, this rule can apply to any amount of money you make. Just because someone makes more money than you do not mean they are worth more than you. The more money you earn, though, the more responsible you must be.

If someone told you that he makes a six-figure income, $100,000 or more, and another person told you he makes $45,000, which person would you say is better off? It is something to think about. The assumption is that the individual that makes $100k is better off because it is thought that you can get everything that you want and need with a six-figure income. Here is an interesting result from research by Purdue University. Researchers found that a salary of $95,000 is ideal to feel satisfied in life, and $60,000 to $75,000 is the range to satisfy our emotional well-being, Inverse.com. These salaries are doable if you want it. However, the dollar amounts mentioned here may not fit you. You must determine what amount of money is suitable for you.

My mother spoke those salaries into existence. When she was alive, she would come and visit with my family occasionally. She would encourage my family through words and actions like good mothers do. As I mentioned earlier, she had a great sense of humor. One time, she told me that my husband was like the government, "He's slow but sure." I never forgot that; it was funny to me. Then on another occasion, she said, "He [my husband] is worth $100,000." The day did come when that happened. As a family, we have always been diligent about our money. Our top two strategies of defense and the cornerstone of our financial lives to live a prosperous life have always been, 1) Make money, 2) Save money. There are other strategies that we have implemented as well. By following our financial plan, when money got funny and we had a financial meltdown, we were able to come through it with no scars.

Your income will partially determine how much you can spend on transportation and housing. You can get a loan from a bank, or you can save up enough money for a vehicle and pay cash for it. You can get a car that "turns heads" and breaks your heart, or you can get a car that is decent and dependable. You should not try and keep up with the Joneses; who are the Joneses anyway?

Transportation and Housing are
Critical to Your Success

Decent transportation and housing are the goal. But with Uber and Lyft, transportation such as a car is not essential. However, it is a good practice to have a car or some mode of transportation that you have quick access to get you from point A to point B. A car is one of the major expenses that you will purchase in your lifetime. I recall getting my first car. My father co-signed the loan for me at our local bank. It was a Buick Skylark sedan that cost $2,000.00. I was 21 years old, working part-time and going to college part-time. When I purchased the car, I did not know that it had a manual shift. So, when the seller brought me the car, I could not even drive it home because I did not know how to drive a stick shift.

Then, entered my mother; she took me to the high school parking lot and taught me how to drive my brand spanking preowned brown Buick Skylark with sunroof, cassette tape player, and soft cushy seats. After 36 months, the terms of the loan, I paid off my loan, and the bank sent me the title of ownership. That major purchase set me on a good course of financial responsibility. Have you made a major purchase? How are you handling it?

A House of Your Own

When I was 29, my husband and I became first-time homeowners. The age is just a reference, some people become homeowners younger and some older. The house was a three-bedroom brick ranch with a basement and an attached garage. It was a 1200 sq. ft. ranch, with beautiful landscaping on a corner lot. If you are thinking of purchasing a home, contact your mortgage company or bank to see how much of a loan you can get. Apply for a loan and get qualified before you look for your dream house so that you will know how much you can spend.

If homeownership is your dream, take advantage of the low mortgage interest rate. With homeowner-ship comes home maintenance, taking care of the lawn, leaky faucet repairs, painting, and yard up-keep, and so on… A home is an investment and will be one of your most prized possessions if you do not buy more house than money. Many people see pur-chasing a home as impossible and unreachable. I want you to do an exercise that will show you the possibility of homeownership. In the next section, track your daily spending.

Track Your Spending, Know Where Every Dime is Going

The purpose of tracking your spending is to find money that you think you do not have. When you track your spending, you will learn a lot about yourself and your spending habits. Write down everything you spend in one day. I know it does not sound like fun, but you must understand that you will be able to control your money better once you discover where it is going. Please do not try and figure it out in your head. There are apps to help you track your spending, but I have done it the old-fashioned way by writing my spending on paper.

Start tomorrow, write down everything you buy, everything you purchase. Write where you made the purchase, what you purchased, and how much it cost. And at the end of the day, before you hit your head on the pillow, before you lay down for a good night's rest, calculate everything you spent that day. It is going to amaze you; you are going to be surprised. I invite you to take this challenge, just try it for three days, just three days. Once you do the tracking of your spending, you are going to be amazed at how much money you have spent (maybe wasted).

Americans are consumers to the bone. Let me say it again, we are consumers to the bone. So, once you discover how much you paid out, it is going to blow you away, and you are going to want to change that habit. So, write it on your calendar, put it on your Google phone or your Yahoo reminder to begin to track everything you purchase that day. Now understand this does not just mean physically going out to make purchases. Make sure you include your online purchases as well. So, if you made a purchase online, you need to write that down and track it too. Got it, that should do it.

Sample Tracking Tool

Purchase	Sun.	M	T	W	Th	F	Sat.
What	Shoes						
Where	Footsies						
When	Aug. 10						
How Much	$45.00						

YouTube Sensations Help Make
Financial Breakthroughs

To learn some life-changing information about managing money, earning money, and investing money, check out three of my favorite YouTube financial gurus. Dave Ramsey (1.78m subscribers), His and Her Money (151k subscribers), and Dr. Lynn Richardson, celebrity financial coach whose biography on YouTube viewed has been 839,380. Each of them provides life-changing information on their YouTube channel. You can turn your financial situation around if you listen to either one of these shows by taking their advice over a significant time period. His and Her Money with Talaat and Tai McNeely, authors and course trainers are the newest to the financial scene, but they are strong contenders. The McNeely's share on one His and Her

Money video, how they paid off their house in 5 years – titled, "We Paid Off Our House In 5 Years!" The main goal is to select two or three experts and stick with them a while, or at least long enough to see a change in your financial situation.

Blessed is the one who always trembles before God, but whoever hardens their heart falls into trouble. – Proverbs 28:14

CHAPTER FOUR

Tell Me About Your God (Higher Power)

God, the creator of the universe. That man who slung the moon into its silvery socket, and the sun in the sky! That man who made the oceans and seas, and separated day from night, the God of all creation. I am talking about the one and only *true and living* God. He died, rose again and is sitting at the right hand of the father soon to return for his bride, the Church. And if you are born again and accepted Jesus Christ as your savior, you will be caught up in the rapture when he returns. But you must be ready when he comes. Matthew 24:42-44, "Therefore, be on the alert, for you do not know which day your Lord is coming. 43 But be sure of this, that if the head of the house had known at what time of the night the thief was coming, he would have been on the alert and would not have allowed his house to be broken into. 44 For this reason you also must be ready; for the Son of Man is coming at an hour when you do not think He will, (ESV)." So, think about it? Who is your God? And if you have never decided to choose a spiritual leader in your life, someone who will lead and guide you and give you counsel and wisdom, now is the time. Search your soul; search your heart; search your mind.

Take the 60 Minute Challenge for God's Sake

You do not have to attend church to accept Jesus Christ. If the doors of the church building never open again, you still have a direct line to the creator; all you have to do is get connected. Here is the challenge. Set aside one hour to be alone. You can accomplish a lot in just one hour. So, prepare in advance for the time that you will spend alone and reaching out to, what some call, a higher power. Go somewhere you cannot be disturbed—the park, leave your house, the basement or the bathroom. Have you seen the commercial with a mother in the bathroom eating cookies and enjoying her privacy, and there is a knock on the door (knock, knock), "Ma!," then she changes her voice with a deep tone to sound like their dad and answers, "It's Dad." Do whatever it takes to protect your privacy. Turn off all social media for just 60 minutes.

Once you have settled on the location, it is time to get down to business. Think about the most difficult time(s) in your life and also think about the most joyous time(s) in your life. In either case, it is probably a miracle that you made it through or that you accomplished something of substance. A miracle is a surprising and welcome event that is not explicable by natural or scientific laws and is therefore considered to be the work of a divine agency, Lexico.com. Repeat the 60-minute challenge once a week, and you will establish a routine with a direct pipeline to the creator, the miracle worker. There may be a time in your life when you need a miracle, so keep the line open.

Meditation (Quiet Please)

Some people do Yoga, others pray, and others sit quietly. Meditation is key to restoration. After you have been beaten up by people who say harsh words or say negative things about you, you need some quiet time. You need time to unwind and restore yourself back to a place of balance. The definition of meditate is to think deeply or focus one's mind for a period, in silence or with the aid of chanting, for religious or spiritual purposes or as a method of relaxation.

Everyone, old and young, needs to meditate because we all have problems. If you have young children, even as young as two years old, teach them now to meditate. Some people call it quiet time. That is right, sit your little one on the floor and look into her eyes and tell her, "Let's focus." Explain to her how people who meditate have a calm, pleasant demeanor. While those who do not focus/meditate, seem to have a high-strung demeanor and are easily upset. Meditation is a way of making you centered and bringing you back to the core. Once you have incorporated meditation into your life, add prayer.

Prayer is a Weapon

Prayer is a weapon. Just like a gun or a knife, prayer is a weapon that you can use to defend yourself against an enemy. With a gun or knife, *you* must fight, but with prayer, *God* fights for you. Which would you rather? Do you want a jail sentence for killing someone or peace in your heart for turning your problem over to an almighty God? You may not have known all of this about prayer, but it is not too late to <u>activate</u> the power of prayer in your life. Let us talk about how easy it is to pray.

First, prayer is communicating with God, either with words or thoughts. You can sit and moan, and he will understand your heart and thoughts. If you want to talk, just simply open your mouth; use the words that come out, say what is on your heart. You will need to address the person you are talking to,

"Dear God." Share what you are thinking about and ask questions about what you are confused about.

Try This Sample Prayer

In Matthew 6:9-13, some call it the "Lord's Prayer," After this manner therefore pray ye: 9 Our Father which art in heaven, Hallowed be they name. 10 Thy kingdom come, Thy will be done in earth, as it is in heaven. 11 Give us this day our daily bread. 12 And forgive us our debts, as we forgive our debtors. 13 And lead us not into temptation but deliver us from evil: For thine is the kingdom, and the power, and the glory, forever. Amen. (KJV)

Why Pray

Prayer is a fundamental practice of Christians. The Bible suggests that we pray always. It is a way to release all the good, the bad and the ugly to the master. One of the most important reasons to pray is to unload secrets that will never be disclosed. If there is something in your life that you do not want anyone to know, tell it to God, if that something will not hurt anyone. However, you should confess your sins or faults to someone who can help you, because you may be carrying something too great to live a healthy life.

We have all sinned and come short of God's glory. No one is better than you, nor is any less than you in the sight of God. Confess your sins so that you can be forgiven. Confession is like removing a weight on your shoulder. Oh, what a relief it is. People sometimes say, "Let me get this off my chest," to indicate that something is bothering them, and they need relief. All I am saying is, if you want life to be easier, pray. Read Dr. Cindy Trimm's 'The

Prayer Warrior's Way' it will set your soul on fire; look her up and check out some of her messages.

Stand, Sit, Kneel When You Pray

Any position is appropriate to pray. Stand, sit or kneel, but more importantly, bring your heart. A quiet room or peaceful place is good. Most recently, since COVID-19, I found a cushion in my home, and I use it to kneel daily to pray. I believe that the intention of the cushion was to be used as a backrest, but I found it to be comforting to kneel on. When you use an object, it is a "point of contact" to connect with God. People use various objects such as "holy water", a handkerchief or a shawl in prayer. Make prayer enjoyable and use your creativity to get your point across.

I have found that mornings work best. Although you can pray throughout the day simply by whispering a word to heaven, you do not always have access to a place where you can go and be quiet, like in the movie, War Room. To have a room solely dedicated to prayer is the ultimate intercessor's dream. In War Room, the actress uses a closet converted to a prayer room. She posted notes on the wall about various situations in her life that she wanted help with. And over time, her requests were answered. The closet was large enough to sit, stand or lay on the floor. This is one movie that I recommend to everyone. You will be thoroughly uplifted and able to Cross-Over after watching the movie.

Perfume and incense bring joy to the heart, and the pleasantness of a friend springs from their heartfelt advice. Proverbs 27:9

CHAPTER FIVE

Tell Me Who Inspires You

———————○———————

T
ell me about the people that inspire you. Many of the people that inspire us are authors. I am going to mention theses globally known authors and see if you have heard of them or their book. Some of the books have been around for a couple decades, and it is okay if you do not recognize them. Dr. Cindy Trimm, The Prayer Warriors Way; T.D. Jakes, 64 Lessons for a Life Without Limits; Dale Carnegie, How to Win Friends and In-

fluence People and The Quick and Easy Way to Effective Speaking; Kenneth Blanchard, Ph.D., The One Minute Manager; Tom Rath, Strengthsfinder 2.0; Suze Orman, The Money Class; Suzan Johnson Cook, Becoming a Woman of Destiny; Joel Osteen, Next Level Thinking; David Bach, Smart Women Finish Rich; Mike Murdock, Seeds of Wisdom on the Word of God; Stedman Graham, Build Your Own Life Brand!; Lilly Walters, Secrets of Superstar Speakers; Joyce Meyer, Approval Addiction and Me and My Big Mouth!; Asha Tyson, How I Retired at 26!, and Dr. Myles Munroe.

Mentor Please

An experienced and trusted adviser advises or trains someone, especially a younger colleague. Ideally, your mentor is someone at your disposal by phone, e-mail, or text. Mentors usually have an extensive schedule, and their calendars are often full, and their time is valuable. It is very common for your mentor to be a teacher, professor, pastor or someone further ahead in your desired career path. Your parents are not your mentors, but they provide a similar type of support that a mentor does.

You will often hear people say that "If it wasn't for (fill in the blank), I wouldn't have made it." Mentors serve you in a variety of ways. They may counsel you about your career, personal matters or finances. Since mentors are very wise individuals who have gained a lot of success and notoriety, make sure that you can take full advantage of them. Also, keep in mind that you need to be honest with your mentor so that their instruction will work in your life.

A Mentor Can Help You CrossOver

So, you want Steve Harvey, comedian, author, game show host and syndicated radio host, as your mentor. You reach out to him and his team and hear nothing back. Steve Harvey has 4.1 million Twitter followers, and he is following 901. The likelihood of you getting Steve as a mentor is very slim. It will be easier to follow him on his social media platforms and purchase his products. According to his Twitter page, he has a store that carries t-shirts, sweatshirts and accessories that will inspire you and make you laugh.

You are more likely to get a local CEO, pastor or teacher as your mentor than Steve Harvey. A local individual can possess as much or more wisdom than a celebrity. Just because an individual is a celebrity does not automatically qualify that individual as a mentor. Wisdom, discernment, skills, experience and training are the components of a good mentor. Your goal will determine which mentor you choose. Now, if you want Dave Bing, former CEO of Bing Steel and Hall of Fame Power Forward for the Detroit Pistons, your chances of getting him is more likely, especially if you live in his neighborhood. Even though he is retired from his corporate job and basketball, he remains active in the community with his non-profit, and you also have a chance of stumbling upon him at the local market.

One of the most likely and qualified persons to get as a mentor who will be available to you by email, text or phone is your teacher/professor. One of the reasons your teacher is best for you is that your goals line up, and you can gain quick access to them. If you are paying college tuition, take advantage of this opportunity. Professors love it when students reach out to them. It makes them feel like they are doing their job and making a difference. Professors welcome questions and feedback from their proteges.

Getting a mentor is not always formal, it just kind of happens sometimes. When you are living your life on purpose, things fall in place for you and the person you need shows up at the right time. The main thing I would say about getting a mentor is, be open to meeting someone new that comes along in your path who has the knowledge that you need to go to the next level.

Oprah Winfrey describes mentorship like this, "A mentor is someone who allows you to see the hope inside yourself."

Honoring Your Parents Comes with Long Life

It is very important to honor your parents because the way you honor your parents is a determin-
ing factor in how long you will live. Tell me who
you honor. Do you honor your parents? The Bible
says that you are to honor your parents so that your
days may be long upon the earth. So, suppose you
have a bad relationship with your parents. If you are
at odds with your parents, it is very crucial to get
that fixed. No matter who is wrong or who is right,
it is necessary to try and come to some resolution.
If your parents are divorced, and you have not re-
covered from that, and you are older now with your
own family, let it go!

As you may know, parents are the first ones to
honor because they brought you here. I have heard
parents say, "I brought you into this world, and I

will take you out." (Laughing). Your adoptive parent or foster parent should be honored and appreciated too. It does not matter who your parent is, you are to give honor to the person who has the authority to make decisions on your behalf as a minor, those who are under the age of 18. However, parents are to be honored no matter what age you are.

Is there a teacher, professor, pastor or mentor in your life? You should always honor somebody who has helped you, planted good seeds in your life or helped you out from a dark place. When you honor someone, you are submitting yourself unto them for leadership and guidance.

The reason why honor is so important is that it puts you in a submissive learning mode to be *taught*. We need people who will protect and guide us in our lives. We need people who love us, and who will love us unconditionally. Some people do not have love in their life. It may be because they are an angry person or an unforgiving person. Honor is very important because you can get to places and move up in your life faster by honoring than by not honoring a person. Mike Murdock, author, preacher and songwriter, has a book that talks about honor, where he says whom you honor is the key to unlocking blessings in your life. Who does not want blessings in their lives? Honor is often done privately, such as sending a card or an email. Honor shows how grateful you are. And when you honor people, they help you CrossOver sooner than later.

Choose my instruction instead of silver, knowledge rather than choice gold, - Proverbs 8:10

CHAPTER SIX

Tell Me What Marketable
Skills You Possess

Whether it is a job or a business of some sort, you must exhibit some marketable skills to make a living. According to Indeed.com, the top three skills that employers look for are Communication, Leadership, and Teamwork (other sources say Customer Service in place of Teamwork). In addition to the three mentioned, these eight make the list of employability skills that human relations staff look for: Interpersonal skills, learning/adaptability skills, self-management skills, organizational skills, computer skills, problem-solving skills, open-mindedness and strong work ethic. Those are the soft skills that get you in the door.

1. You may be highly skilled with certifications and possess a degree. Still, if you are lacking in the essential employable skills, you may not be the candidate of choice. Let us examine these skills and what they mean and find out if you possess them or not. 1) Communication – how you relate through talking or speaking to others. Do you speak with confidence and use proper English? For example, do you say "Hello" or "Hey"? Hello, is more appropriate and professional. That is just one example. And do you used eye contact when communicating with people? For an exercise,

record your voice and listen very closely to how you enunciate words. Make sure you are pronouncing the letter "t" in words. I know we have all made the mistake of saying "dat" instead of "that."

2. Leadership – stepping up to be the one who will get the answer that is needed at the time and making decisions during chaos. True leaders are servants first. They are happy to take charge and help others in tough times, as well as take responsibility for failures. Leaders do not back down in challenging moments nor hide amid confusion. Suppose a disgruntled customer comes in your store and says to you, "You told me to do it this way, and the item broke." There are ways to settle your customer down and have a satisfied customer

in the end. A leader who knows how to empathize and yet remain firm will have the greatest impact on the outcome. Listen, assess, and decide. I call it the L.A.D. approach.

3. Teamwork – believe it or not, teamwork is not the easiest skill to possess. Some personalities are more introverted and used to working alone. Some personalities are selfish and bossy. Is that you? Teamwork is when you join a common goal and assist your teammates in reaching the goal. The opportune word is assisting. For example, if your coworker is running late for work and an internal customer comes looking for something that your coworker is familiar with, but you step in to assist, that's teamwork. Teamwork means to put pride aside and humble yourself

to create an atmosphere of care, safety, and support for each other.

4. Interpersonal skills - knowing how to communicate with people. Giving proper respect to others and professionally handling matters. The fundamentals of interpersonal skills are giving a listening ear to another and communicating effectively. For example, saying "Thank you" and "Please," also hearing another out and what they have to say. Effective communication is learned, and with practice, you get better at it. It is not obvious how to communicate but it is good manners, which is a learned behavior also.

5. Self-management skills - getting yourself to work on time and being productive. Can you motivate yourself to properly carry out what

needs to be done? And do you know or anticipate what needs to be accomplished. Putting things in the right perspective. Not always needing someone to manage you. Being self-motivated. Count yourself blessed if you possess this skill because there are many distractions in the world today with COVID-19 and the protest going on after the death of George Floyd.

6. Organizational skills – making things easy to find to accomplish the task at hand. Using a filing system of some sort to keep organized. Folders are still a good way to keep papers organized for home and work. In a nutshell, organizational skills are the equivalent of finding something quickly when you need it. My husband always says, "Put it back where you found it." And that is all folks!

7. Computer skills – doesn't everyone know how to use a computer? Knowledge of using computer software programs such as Microsoft Word, Excel and PowerPoint is helpful for most desk jobs. The computer is essential in today's job market because all businesses use the computer in some fashion. Technology has brought us a long way. I remember when I was working for the government and our department first transitioned to computers. One lady in our department that I was working with resisted and complained about using the computer. Our team eventually learned the system and we appreciated the efficiency it brought.

8. Problem-solving skills – when you can solve a problem, you can plan. Solving problems

moves you closer to your goal. Problem-solving is when you can take a situation and dissect the components then reasonably conclude what works. A problem solver knows how to solicit the team to get to the bottom of every situation. When something needs to be done, and the task seems too difficult or large, problem solvers step up and say, "We'll get this done, whatever it takes." Inventors are problem solvers who have made our lives easier. Inventions like the shovel, cell phone, sewing machine, microwave oven, air conditioning, computer, lights, concrete, umbrellas… and the list goes on. What problem have you solved lately?

9. Open-mindedness – is a skill that says, I appreciate what you bring to the table. The world is too big and filled with opportunities

all around us to be closed-minded. When you are open-minded, more opportunities come toward you. You take the limits off life being open-minded. Your goal is to dream the unthinkable and do the impossible. Open-minded people make the world a better place. Being open-minded does not mean that you have no standards, that is far from the truth. In fact, you have high standards and great expectations. So, keep an open mind, you just might inspire someone.

10. Strong work ethic – I was shopping at a well-known discount store the other day and noticed some inconsistencies in the store. As I proceeded to leave the store, I asked the manager what had happened. Her response to me was that she just started working there a few days ago, and the previous manager quit

without giving notice and left with the keys to the store. The store was quite a mess. It looked to be in disarray, disorganized and un-kept—not a strong work ethic presence at all. The bottom line is do the right thing!

When you have a strong work ethic, you are de-pendable, and you put in a full day's work for a full day's pay. You do not act out of character just be-cause no one's watching. Do you take pride in your work? Do you complete your assignments and ask for more? This may seem elementary, but to get to the next grade, you must pass the elementary test. You are ahead of the game with this skill, stay strong. You are practically guaranteed a good job and move up in the organization if you have a strong work ethic.

Dream Job / Career

So, what is your dream job or dream career? Since the pandemic, coupled with the social injustice marches, I see great opportunities to do something that you really enjoy doing. For example, if you participated in the protest, there are many opportunities to do something like what you did when you were protesting for pay. Whether you marched or stayed at home and advocated for victims of racial injustice, there is something for you to do. Here is a list of occupations you may want to consider: you can be an artist, speaker, photographer or police. You can start your own home-based business. You can be an event planner or event coordinator. You can be a social media guru. You can be a YouTube sensation. You can be a shoe designer or a mask maker. Mental health, social and medical field workers are needed. As you can see, the opportunities are unlimited. I have included a table to show you several jobs and careers with potential to be in demand in the future as the economy has shifted. A great career will help you CrossOver.

Career / Business	Average USA Salary	Source
Audio Engineer	$26.85	Indeed.com
Artist – (Drawing)	$22.00/hr. - $44,898	ZipRecruiter
Author	$0.00 – Six figures	Author
Beverage Distributor	$45,033	Indeed.com
CSR Customer Service Rep (Remote)	$14.15/hr.	payscale.com
EMT (Emergency Medical Technician)	$24,000 - $33,000	ZipRecruiter
Footwear Designer (Developer)	$60,865	Glassdoor.com

Instagram (Influencer)	Under 10,000 followers - $88.00 per post; 80,000 followers - $200.00 per post	Petalcard.com
Face Mask Maker / Seller	Data not available	N/A
Motivational Speaker	$10,000 - $300,000 Range	Motivationalspeakerz.com
News Anchor	$38,647	Indeed.com
Photographer	$30,000 - $40,000 Average Range	Photomba.net
Police Officer	$53,830 Annually	Indeed.com
Politician (City, County, State)	$50,000+ City Council (highest pay)	Naples, Fl local paper
Script Writer	$28.50/hr.	Bureau of Labor Statistics
Security Window Business	Unlimited	Author
Shuttle Service (Transportation)	$15 - $25/hr.	Salary.com
Sign Maker – Digital and Hand Printing	$50 - $60/hr.	Howtostartanllc.com

Street Cleaner	$25,000 - $35,500	ZipRecruiter.com
Teacher	$41,110	Wolfram Alpha
T-Shirt Shop Owner	$100,000 Annually	Screenprinting-aspa.com
Tour Guide	$15.75/hr. ($75 tips per day)	Indeed.com
Tutor	$17.81	payscale.com
Videographer	$65,957 Annually	Salary.com
YouTuber (Influencer)	$5 per 1000 views; $5,000 per 1,000,000	Google.com

Those who control their anger have great under-

standing; those with a hasty temper will make mis-

takes. – Proverbs 14:29

CHAPTER SEVEN

Tell Me What Makes You Angry

T he late Dr. Myles Munroe, motivational speaker, author and pastor, taught that what makes you angry is an indication to what you are called to do. What angers you does not necessarily anger someone else. Take notice of the things that anger you and see how often the same thoughts come up in your life. Anger is not a bad thing in its proper context. Anger is the reason that we have many freedoms that we enjoy—someone fought for our rights. Anger is simply a signal that something is wrong or that something bothers you, and you should address it before it gets the best of you.

Great songs have been written because someone was angry. Kirk Franklin, songwriter and producer, wrote I Smile. The song starts out with, "I dedicate this song to recession, depression and unemployment. This song's for you..." Paintings have been produced out of anger. Great scripts have been written out of anger. Tyler Perry, considered the highest-paid person in entertainment, is a great example of someone who pressed through his anger to become a mogul. Perry created the character Madea which is rooted in his goal for people to treat women right. In life, your goal is to be a problem solver, but you need to get to the root of your anger. The better able you are to problem solve, the better your life will be because you will be rewarded for your problem-solving ability. And money is the reward for problem solving.

Anger is a natural response to things that bother us. And it is okay to be angry but not to the extent where it hinders or harms your health. The Bible says to be angry and sin *not*. The Bible also says, "Do not let the sun go down on your wrath." So, do not let your anger linger. I know that you probably know people who hang on to unforgiveness for years. Maybe you are holding on to something troubling you right now. The interesting thing about anger is that we may not even know that we are angry. Unfortunately, anger is very strong. But positivity and hopeful thinking can snuff out anger. You must desire the good in life to be able to receive goodness. Learn why you are angry and find constructive ways to address the things that bother you.

Solve a Problem Immediately

I am sure you have seen signs posted on small business establishments such as, "Hiring, Apply Within, Job Openings Now" and so forth. Apply within connotates that there is no waiting period and that the competition is low. All you need to do is walk in to be considered. If you are a person who wants to get results now, then I am talking to you. There was a time when it took weeks and several days, sometimes, months to get offered a position. But in today's climate, you can land a job opportunity immediately! And when you see this sign, do not hesitate to dive in immediately to claim your territory. You will be solving a problem and making a difference in your community. You have no good reason to put off your dreams any longer, so apply within. You must start somewhere.

Huge Sign "Hiring"

When a company is hiring, there may be a waiting period, which is okay if you need to get things in order. The definition of hiring means it is an on-going event. Not a one-time event. They could be hiring today, tomorrow, or even several months down the road. You often see this sign on fast food restaurant windows, retail stores, grocery stores and places of business that offer services. Major stores, "Big Box Stores" are usually fast-paced, and you most likely will have to deal with lots of people and products. If you are high-energy and like your day to go by quickly, this job is waiting for you. Take notice of the companies that have increased their minimum wage.

Job Openings Now

Sometimes "Job Openings Now" is an indication that it is a production or commission job that needs lots of people. This job may require you to work in a warehouse or telemarketing. Jobs that are in constant need are jobs with high turnover rates. However, high turnover could indicate an opportunity for advancement. If you are in the field or industry you want to be in, you should consider taking this job to learn about the role. There is nothing wrong with starting at the bottom if there is a stairway to the top. More importantly, try and stick with the job for six months to a year. Give yourself and the job a chance to grow. You never know, it could be a sweet marriage.

If you think that job hopping does not affect your opportunities, think again. The Balance Careers website reported The Bullhorn survey and what hiring managers say about placing applicants; "A 58-year-old with a steady employment history is *easier* to place than a thirty-year-old job hopper." So, there you have it!

COVID-19 Opportunities

During COVID-19, non-essential businesses were ordered to close as the governors of many states entered executive orders. Non-essential businesses are considered "recreational" in nature, the Business Insider. The following types of businesses are considered non-essential: Theaters, gyms and recreation centers, salons and spas, museums, casinos and racetracks, shopping malls, bowling alleys and sporting and concert venues. One in seven businesses is expected to close for good.

Here is a report of the status of 12 small businesses in a shopping plaza on one corner of God's earth after two months of being in a pandemic, 60 days following the shut-down of local businesses during the pandemic:

Type of Business	Open or Closed
Hebrew Book Store	**Open**
MRI	**Open**
Cell Phone Store	Closed
Hobby Store	**Open (Curbside)**
Cleaners (Laundry)	**Open**
3 Restaurants: Chinese, Coney Island, and Seafood	**Open (Carry Out Only)**
Beauty Salon	Closed
Retail Boutique	Closed
Eyebrow Salon	Closed
Shoe Repair Shop	Closed

The previous report gives you something to think about if you want to start your own business someday.

You Are NOT the Boss of Me
- I am My Own Boss

That sounds so good, am I right? Say it with me, "I'm my own boss." Are you ready for all the paperwork? The long days and long nights? And please do not tell me that you can make X amount of dollars working only three to five hours a week. The business owners who are working only three to five hours per week did not start out like that. They built up a clientele strong enough to sit back and reap the rewards of their labor. There is a bright side to being your own boss, though. You have the flexibility of not having a strict schedule, but you better believe that you must be consistent to maintain your business. In the previous chapter, I listed several jobs and career opportunities. I want you to revisit the list and decide which type of business fits your style. Is it a medical facility, hobby store, cleaners or a restaurant?

Small Business vs. Home-Based Business

A small business employs 1 – 50 people and can be off-site or a brick and mortar store. A home-based business is a business that you operate based out of your home. You are the employee, and it is usually located in a designated area of the house, maybe an office. Both businesses afford you certain tax write-offs. According to Dr. Lynn Richardson, and I am a fan of hers, she urges everyone to have a home-based business. She notes that there are 475 potential tax write-offs that a home-based business can take advantage of. Sounds like a great idea. I have personally taken advantage of having a home-based business as a Freelancer. I have contracted my writing services out to many venues. Most of the income I received in my home-based businesses provided additional income for my family. There are other opportunities to earn income and are referred to as a "Side Hustle."

A Side Hustle Can Pick Up the Slack

If your part-time or full-time job does not create the income that you want or need, you can get a side hustle. Let me explain the definition of a side hustle. It is something that you do alongside your main job. Although it is true that you can turn your side hustle into full-time money-making, beware of the scams that claim you will earn lots of money in a short amount of time. I will save you from the scammer. But only you can decide.

Here are a few tried and true side hustles that have endured for many years. My personal favorite is: 1) eBay seller. eBay is probably one of the longest standing legitimate and doable side hustles in the world. And it has a very quick cash flow turn-a-round. If you have something new or preowned in excellent condition, you could be making money selling it on eBay. 2) Freelance Writing on Hub-Pages. If you are a good writer and are consistent in writing as well as commenting, then you will do well on this site. HubPages is like having a blog, and you can monetize it. You can write about topics that you enjoy or have experience as an expert. If you love traveling and have traveled more than the average person, this could be a good topic for you. Another great thing about HubPages is, if you enjoy taking photos, you can put those photos to good use on HubPages, and 3) Mystery shopping. Do you love critiquing retail businesses and have a vehicle? You will do well at this job. You need to have a very flexible schedule because opportunities are usually at various times of the day and week. But you can make a decent amount of money if you are consistent. Research for demand. Lastly, a huge way to address your anger about the world's condition and our economy is to open a business, especially if you are African American.

Black-Owned Business

Restaurants, hair salons/barbershops and clothing stores are the most popular businesses in the black community and the most popular ones that blacks own. So, when blacks come to our hobby store and learn that the owner is black, they light up and smile. Sometimes the black African American customers tell us they "love" us after we provide the service they want. We get just as much appreciation from many of the Caucasian patrons too. Since the day the hobby store opened, several African Americans come in, asking the question, "Is this Black-owned?" Black businesses empower black people. It makes them feel proud, valued, and a part of this big world.

Growing up as a little girl around the age of eight, my mother used to take me to a local laundromat that was black owned. I do not remember the name of it, but Mr. McLaurin was the proprietor. On our side of town, there were several black-owned businesses. There was a restaurant named The Shrimp Hut, which was black owned as well. On Fridays, my dad would treat us to a bucket of fried chicken and a pound or two of shrimp, and man, it was delicious. There was also a Dime store owned by the Barnetts, where we purchased our bolo bat and jacks from. And Blacks Men's Clothing store. When blacks are built up and empowered, the community is empowered. That was a lot of information about jobs, careers and businesses, so keep your book nearby as a resource when trying to climb that ladder of success.

All hard work brings a profit, but mere talk leads only to poverty. Proverbs 14:23

CHAPTER EIGHT

Tell Me What You Do in Your Free Time

———————o———————

I s there something that you used to do when you were a child that you would like to pick up again? As a child, I grew up playing the bolo bat; today, it is called paddle ball. My mother taught me how to bolo bat at a very young age. I was about the age of seven when I learned to play paddle ball. Some 50 years later, I picked up the paddle ball again and began to practice. After all those years, just 20 minutes of practice, I was playing paddle ball once again.

At the hobby store, I am endearingly known as the First Lady. As a brand ambassador, using the paddle ball allows me to leverage that skill into something greater. Many customers come in to find things for their children. And you guessed it, I introduce them to the paddle ball. Since the store has been open, in my estimation, I have taught, showed or demonstrated the paddle ball to approximately 1,000 people. Do you understand where I am going with this? Your hobby, your skills and abilities outside of your job can enhance your total life experience and even increase your income. So, do not take your hobby for granted.

Your free time is meant to be stress-free, so do not work your hobby like a job. "Sometimes when you turn a hobby into a job, it becomes work." – Jeff Bennett. A hobby can be classified as something that you do that is not work-related to relax and/or for enrichment. In our hobby store, people come from all walks of life to get products and accessories for the hobbies that they enjoy. And there is no age limit on hobbies. In fact, you can learn a hobby and turn it into a career. If you choose to, you can do a hobby that is job-related. For example, one of our customers enjoys remote control cars, and he is a mechanic. Another individual comes for paint, and he is an artist.

Since people are spending more time at home, because of the COVID-19 safety orders, the puzzle business has soared. Puzzles come in all shapes and sorts, and in various amounts of pieces. One of the most common number of pieces is the 1000-piece puzzle. That may seem like a lot to you, but if you are a real aficionado, 1000 pieces is a common amount to construct. Do not be surprised if your friends and family do not enjoy hobbies like you. It is a great opportunity to enhance your life. Hobbies are a great discussion piece, great for conversation and great for relieving stress. A hobby should be treated just like exercise. You should practice it regularly and do it often to get the greatest benefit from it.

Since I have reconnected with the paddle ball, I am now able to do 200 paddles consecutively in one session. I hit the ball 2.75 times every second. You can call me the Paddle Ball Queen. I have introduced the paddle ball to children's groups, adults who love old school games and anyone who wants to have fun.

I hope you recall the experience that you enjoyed growing up as a child. And if you used to have fun doing it, think about returning to it or getting a new hobby. Another great thing that a hobby can do for you is, it can be your career. My husband has a slogan that says, "A hobby is an inroad to a career."

Please do not allow anyone to knock your hobby. You might knit or crochet. Do calligraphy or paint. It does not matter what your hobby is, what matters is that you are doing something constructive to enrich your life in your free time. "The idle brain is the devil's workshop." Do you recall the boy who would scribble and doodle on his homework and papers? His name is Joseph Whale, and he was only 9 years old when he was discovered for his artistic ability to doodle. In fact, he was so good that a restaurant hired him to doodle on their walls. The walls of the restaurant look like it was professionally designed. It was Joseph's parents who noticed his unique ability and enrolled him in an afterschool program to enhance his ability. So, do not mock small beginnings.

The Ultimate Prize

When you can arise each morning and have a sense of fulfillment and can look yourself in the mirror with a smile on your face, you can then be at peace with yourself and this world. You were born to WIN! You are a fighter, not a quitter. Do not worry if your friends do not support you, they probably cannot even help themselves. And do not believe the hype that you see on social media, everyone has trouble in their life. Life is not worth you trying to gain someone else's support by giving up who you are. You are number one! Live your life like a protester and fight in heat, cold, rain, sweat, sore feet and all. Fight for yourself until you almost pass out. What do the airlines tell you on a flight? Get your oxygen mask *first*, then help someone else.

If you want to CrossOver, you must do all that you can. Here is how Les Brown says it.

"Choosing Your Future"

If you want a thing bad enough

To go out and fight for it

To Work day and night for it

To give up your time, your peace

And your sleep for it,

If all that you dream and scheme

Is about it

And life seems useless and worthless without it

And if you gladly sweat for it,

And fret for it, And plan for it

And lose all your terror of the opposition for it

And if you simply go after that thing that you want

With all of your capacity

Strength and sagacity

Faith, hope and confidence

And stern pertinacity

If neither cold poverty,

Famish or gull

Sickness or pain

Or body and brain

Can keep you away from the thing that you want

If darker than grim

You besiege and beset it

With the help of God

You will get it!

   - Les Brown

Be sure to know the condition of your flocks, give careful attention to your herds. Proverbs 27:23

CHAPTER NINE

Tell Me About Your Image

B eyoncé is a talented and beautiful singer, dancer and actress. That was easy to say. I wonder, can people describe you that easily? Your life should be so loud that it is undeniably you. Your scent should be so loud that people smell your personality at a distance. When Beyoncé takes the stage with her backup dancers, they come out in step, in sync, high stepping to entertain you. Your image is how people see you. For example, they may see you as professional, sophisticated, or they may view you in a negative light, such as a liar or gossip. What is your preferred view of yourself? Everything about you says who you are. From the way you dress to the way you speak, and even the way you physically move.

Do You Light Up the Room?

When you enter a room, what response do you get from the people that are there? Are they happy to see you or are they disappointed? Do they have a smile on their face or is there a frown on their face? Take notice of how people respond to you when you enter a room. I want people to feel happy and loved when I am around them. Have you ever watched Showtime at the Apollo? The show is based on contestants who bring their act to the stage in front of a large audience, in hopes of winning the grand prize.

As the contestants perform their skill, singing, dancing or comedy, the audience responds. The various acts will get approval by the audience cheering, clapping or standing. At other times, the contestant will get a negative response, such as booing or the audience asking the contestant to leave. Usually, the audience gets it right and nails it by selecting the best participant. So, ask yourself are people cheering or booing for me. Your answer might be found in your apparel.

Pajamas in Public

It seems that today, anything goes when it comes to attire. I never thought that I would see the day when people come out in public and go shopping dressed in their pajamas and house shoes. Some lingerie indeed looks appropriate to wear outdoors.

But lingerie is appropriate for the house, the bedroom, relaxing or on vacation in a hotel room. Pajamas are an intimate item and you want to keep them that way. Keep them in good condition so that they remain sanitary and sacred. Now, if you are a model and you are making money, then this is a great opportunity to make a commercial. Some people may argue and say, "Oh well, people don't have to look at me, they can look in another direction." But it is usually too late to look in another direction once you have been seen. The bottom line is, you can wear whatever you want wherever you go, just be ready for the response and the consequences of your actions.

Dress Your Best

Clean, neat, ironed, pressed and smelling fresh! Dress daily as if you are going to be interviewed.

The suit and tie or dress and heels are not at the top of the list for being interviewed these days. If you have something that is neat clean and has no rips or tears, you are good to go. For men or a young man, a dress shirt is appropriate, a tie is more fitting for a corporate interview. For ladies or young ladies, slacks or skirt, a collared blouse and business casual shoes are appropriate for an interview. For interviews that are conducted on Skype, you still need to dress up. And make sure you are wearing bottoms. (Laugh).

Did you hear about the anchor who only wore a shirt and no pants during his segment of a show? Since this pandemic, many anchors work from home, and you can only see what they are wearing above the waist. But there was this one anchor who decided not to wear any bottoms, it was hilarious to learn about this. A survey reported that sales have gone up for shirts and tops because people were having more Zoom meetings and conference calls from home, and participants are not wearing bottoms because their waist is not disclosed in a typical conference call. The best thing to do about the dress code when going to an interview is to ask ahead of time to be sure of what you should wear. When you look good, you feel good.

Laughter Just Like a Medicine

What is your constant state of mind? Pleasant, cheerful, helpful, kind and knowledgeable are a few character traits that come to mind. Are you hopeful or are you dismayed? A cheerful heart does good like a medicine, Proverbs. There is a song by BeBe Winans called, "Laughter Just Like A Medicine."

This song has become very popular, and he sang it with four young Korean men. It is a beautiful song that makes you think about your attitude. I can just hear it in my head right now as I think about the lyrics.

Eat to Live vs. Live to Eat

What do you put in your temple? Your temple (body) is the Lord's. The things that you eat or drink will reflect in your health, as well as other areas of your life. In our health-conscious world, there are many opportunities to be a healthy person. You can be a vegetarian, a vegan, someone that does not eat meat or someone on a *see* food diet – eat everything you see! When you awake in the morning, are you full of life or are you sluggish? If you are sluggish, something is going on in your body that you need to address. 1 Corinthians 6:19 -20 19 Do you not know that your bodies are temples of the Holy Spirit, who is in you, whom you have received from God? 20 You were bought at a price. Therefore, honor God with your bodies. Your daily diet is key to your health.

Nick Cannon, The Masked Singer show host, actor, rapper, comedian, writer and producer, BS Howard University, is a prime example of someone who stays fit. He has an elaborate gym and a personal trainer that he works out with. Nick has a health condition that must be monitored for him to stay healthy. As you can see, money does not make a person immune to health issues.

He who finds a wife finds a good thing and obtains favor from the Lord. – Proverbs 18:22 ESV

CHAPTER TEN

Tell Me Your Thoughts on Marriage

The institution of marriage was established at the beginning of time. Marriage is the backbone and glue to society because out of it stems children. If you are not married or opposed to marriage, you must have a good reason. If you are opposed to getting married, it poses a threat and a concern for our communities to thrive and grow. Many couples have decided to live with a partner rather than get married. In 2020 there are more couples living together than in the 80s. I often think about young people today and how their relationships are thriving or not. There seems to be a breakdown in communication and a lack of the ability to compromise. There should be a class or a course about marriage in every school starting at the high school level to train students about marriage.

It is interesting that schools teach sex education but do not teach about marriage. It has been scientifically proven that two parents can raise a child better than one. It is true that a child needs both a mother and a father. And yet there are many single moms. In one of the largest cities in the country, Detroit, Michigan, the single parent head of household constitutes 70% of the population. And more than 50% of the households in the urban area of Detroit is run by women. Women may do a good job, but fathers are needed.

Kobe Bryant Was a Great Father

A high number of fathers in the black community fall into the categories of early death, incarceration, gay or absent (disowning a child). Some men are also impoverished. And many people do not know who their biological father is. It is difficult to be a father if you do not know your own father. However, there are great examples of what an excellent father looks like who has Crossed Over.

Kobe Bryant, one of the greatest basketball players ever to live, set the bar super high in the fatherhood department. After Kobe was tragically killed, his life became one of the most inspirational platforms for the world to see. I get chills just thinking about the wonderful legacy that he left for his daughters and his wife. Even though he and his wife wanted a boy, they were extremely happy to have and raise daughters. His ability to parent and be a great father set him apart as one of the greatest fathers of all time. Even though he has gone down in history as one of the best basketball players ever to live, he fathered at that same level.

We can learn a lot about the life Kobe lived in the way that he loved his children. You might say, "Oh, he was rich." That I will agree, make no mistake about it. But to look into his eyes, money had nothing to do with the way he loved his daughters. Money does not make you spend time with your children; your heart and having a responsible attitude causes you to spend time training, teaching and loving your children. Even though he and his wife raised beautiful daughters, they did have problems and challenges just like everyone else. But one thing about life is that if you keep on at it with a good attitude, you will succeed. So, Kobe, thank you for showing the world what a great father looks like.

Is Marriage for you?

Many people cannot answer this question with an immediate yes. The reasons vary as much as the people who answer the question. Some have been married once before; some do not see a need, and others are still hurt from previous relationships and are stuck. If you understand the biblical rational behind marriage, then marriage is probably right for you. Read Ephesians 5:22 – 33. A man must be able to leave his father and mother and be united to his wife, and they become one flesh. A man must first love his wife as he loves himself and the wife must respect her husband. Those instructions are the basics of marriage. Marriage is for mature individuals and if you cannot agree at the base level, then marriage is not right for you. Two are better than one though. Finally, if you will submit to God then you will be able to submit to your spouse.

Marriage for Dummies 101

Since I have been married over three decades, I think I am qualified to give you some good advice on how to have a successful marriage. No, my marriage is not perfect, but it is sweet, solid, and still thriving. One of the longest living married couples that I personally know have been married for 65 years. They have been married almost twice as long as my husband and I. Think about that for a moment. They both worked, raised children, had successful careers and have grandchildren too. Together they impacted the community, their neighborhood and their grandchildren. So, from their relationship and my personal experience, I will share with you three of the greatest things to having a good solid marriage that you can enjoy. Lesson number one never give up. Lesson number two your spouse is the number one person in your life that you share everything with, not your friend. Lesson number three work together as a team to accomplish great things in your life. You probably thought there was a complicated lesson.

Really, the main thing that keeps a marriage thriving is constantly working on yourself. Be the example to your spouse that you want for yourself. Do not expect your spouse to be perfect. We live in an imperfect world with imperfect people. Do not depend on your spouse for your happiness. You oversee your own life and how to get what you want out of it. That does not mean that you do not need your spouse, it means that you enhance the marriage. Marriage is not a fairytale; it is not a movie. It is real—alive and breathing. Treat your marriage like a rare jewel or a diamond. Polish it, shine it and do not let anybody in it that is not helping to improve it! At the first indication that someone close to you does not respect your spouse or talks against your spouse, let that person go. Remove that person from your life immediately.

The Real Purpose of Dating

I know already, it is complicated! You are unemployed, it is hard to find an honest person and your last relationship went sour. I almost wish that there was a license for dating. Dating is so misunderstood, and the purpose of dating seems to have been dummied down. When you get to the point that you want to date someone, you should have marriage on your mind. Dating is a prelude to marriage. And friendship is the prelude to dating. There, I have just cleared up the matter of dating. Friendship must be established before you can progress into a serious relationship. Friendship is what seems to be missing in many of the relationships I have come across.

Friendship is The Foundation for a Relationship

Remember when you were in grade school or high school, and you had a crush on the cutest guy in the class? You kept your distance until such time came that you could make a move. You may have waited until in between class periods and you were walking to your next class, or you may have waited until the end of the school day to ask for his phone number. Whatever the case may be, you started with a shy hello, a polite request for his phone number and a phone call to chat. You kept your distance until you got to know the person you were thinking about. When you maintain your relationships at a friendship level, you have just saved yourself a whole lot of drama. Friendship is a special fun time in a relationship, and it is the foundation for building a marriage. To sum up the whole marriage process, friendship helps you crossover into dating and dating helps you crossover into marriage.

It is my hope that I have shed some light on your situation and that you will be able to reach higher heights and go to deeper depths. All of the questions and discussion in this book were designed to help you CrossOver into a place of fulfillment in life. The content helps you to grow and become independent of your parent, and you can come back time and again to review the information that you have read and eventually pass it on to your child or some-one you love! Thank you for reading and stay tuned for my next book to help grow your business.

CROSSOVER PRAYER

Dear God, I thank you for every young person, every parent, every counselor and every other individual who has read this book. I pray that from this day forward, you would help them to cross over to the impossible dream. I know that there is nothing too hard for you. I thank you for everyone who has come to get clarity and understanding and wisdom for their life. I pray your blessing on their finances, their mental and spiritual health, and their physical health. You are a way maker. You are our source of life, and without you, we are nothing. Every breath

that we breathe is because you allow it. So, again, I
thank you for those who have come for help, and I
pray that they will CrossOver and take others with
them too.

ABOUT THE AUTHOR

Sima Ballinger is a Dale Carnegie honors graduate of the Effective Speaking and Human Relations Course and holds a B.B.A. from Davenport University. Sima is the First Lady of HobbyTown (Southfield), where she is a Brand Ambassador while her husband is the owner. She is the author of "Paddle Ball with Me: Learn to Paddle Ball like a Pro in 5 Simple Steps," an illustrated guide of the bounce back paddle ball (bolo bat). She can paddle 200 times non-stop, and her Paddle Ball Program has taught many girls and boys: confidence, hand-eye-coordination and to incorporate exercise in their lives. On HubPages, her most popular Hub, "10

Characteristics of a Passionate Person," has been viewed more than 71,000 times, and "How to be a Great MC, Moderator and Host," 25,000 times. As a Ghost Writer, she wrote for a nationally known celebrity's coaching program. She is a former Team Leader for the University of Michigan, Institute for Social Research, Survey Research Center. During the Moving to Opportunity (MTO) Project, her team consistently performed in the top five percent throughout its almost two-year operation. Sima resides in Southfield, Michigan with her husband Marvin Ballinger, and they have three adult children, Virginia, Benjamin and Jasper. Sima's mantra is, People will overlook your lack of knowledge, but not your lack of passion. Connect with Sima: Facebook: HobbyTown (Southfield); Facebook: Sima Beard Ballinger or email:

Simaballinger@yahoo.com

Made in the USA
Columbia, SC
28 October 2020